CW01594503

POETRY ESCAPE

POEMS FROM THE WEST MIDLANDS

Edited By Jenni Harrison

First published in Great Britain in 2019 by:

Young Writers Est. 1991

Young Writers
Remus House
Coltsfoot Drive
Peterborough
PE2 9BF
Telephone: 01733 890066
Website: www.youngwriters.co.uk

Book Design by Ashley Janson

SB ISBN 978-1-78988-198-1
Printed and bound in the UK by BookPrintingUK
Website: www.bookprintinguk.com
YB0392V

FOREWORD

Since 1991 our aim here at Young Writers has been to encourage creativity in children and young adults and to inspire a love of the written word. Each competition is tailored to the relevant age group, hopefully giving each student the inspiration and incentive to create their own piece of creative writing, whether it's a poem or a short story. We truly believe that seeing their work in print gives students a sense of achievement and pride.

For our latest competition Poetry Escape, we challenged secondary school students to free their creativity and escape the maze of their minds using poetic techniques as their tools of navigation. They had several pathways to choose from, with each one offering either a specific theme or a writing constraint. Alternatively they could forge their own route, because there's no such thing as a dead end where imagination is concerned.

The result is an inspiring anthology full of ideas, hopes, fears and imagination, proving that creativity really does offer escape, in whatever form you need it.

We encourage young writers to express themselves and address topics that matter to them, which sometimes means exploring sensitive or difficult topics. If you have been affected by any issues raised in this book, details on where to find help can be found at: **www.youngwriters.co.uk/support.**

CONTENTS

Oswestry School, Oswestry

Pedmore High School, Stourbridge

Q3 Academy, Tipton

Smith's Wood Academy, Smith's Wood

Tenbury High Ormiston Academy, Tenbury Wells

THE POEMS

GREAT STUFF

FIFA is great
Football is fun
I play out with my mates
I love to run.

Fortnite is amazing
It has me and my friends gazing
Food makes me happy
My dog is yappy.

Harvey Mclean (13)

THE YEAR 10,000

I remember the day I was born,
2018, when I entered the world
And I'm still alive in a robot.
It's the year 10,000,
Things I've seen and done have made me better,
Stronger, happier and more loving.
In 2020, I said my first word 'momma'.
Who knew we would be living on Mars
With no cars or troopers rolling around!
In 2030, the PS6 came out,
I've done nothing but play,
Every day, nothing to say.
Now in the year 10,000, we have all this,
A KdP 4, the best of consoles.
In 2090, I got a portal gun
And had lots of fun,
But now, it's the portal x9.
In the year 2100, robots were launched
And I become one still alive,
Still with all the memories.
I didn't have friends growing up,
All I had was family and YouTube.
In the year 10,000, YouTube is no longer a thing,
My mom and dad,
The best I had,
They were born in 1990 and they're still here,

There's no king or queen because we're living on Mars.

It's the year 10,000 and I'm logging out...

Haiden Gittins (12)
Bloxwich Academy, Leamore

AN ODE TO THE UNKNOWN

Your future light burns grey
Green no more; blue no more
Even though your pain is at bay
And that there is nothing left to endure
The blue that is left still waves
And the green may grow more
Despite all of this, they're left in their graves
With nothing left to endure.

Is this what you wanted?
To feel the green go ablaze
To feel yourself rot and become distorted
And for that blue to raise
Your dances have halted
You spin for me no more
And at this time, the impetuous have faulted...
We mourn your disappearance, but can we say so?
It is our fault; I wish I knew the unknown.

Grace Hawkins (13)
Bloxwich Academy, Leamore

MY FEELINGS

These feelings inside my brain
Are making me go insane.
All it takes is a bit of anger
And I'm being dragged down
Like my body is an anchor.
Then a tiny bit of anxiety,
Which is not at all exciting.

Then two tablespoons of happiness
That takes away all the pappiness,
Then loads of love
That'll make you feel so loved.
After all of that, add two tablespoons of patience
And then wait for the bang, then the quietness.

Everyone has mixed emotions,
Just like you and me.
Some can be happy and some can be sad,
But I am always glad
That I am not always feeling sad.

Ellie-May Bates (12)
Bloxwich Academy, Leamore

THE FUTURE IS CLOSER THAN YOU THINK

The future is a clear mystery
As no one knows what will happen.
Maybe aliens will be found on Mars?
As days pass, people wonder...
How are we even alive?

People died in 1940 but what if
The people of the past knew that we would exist?
As they left us their treasures and stuff,
Pyramids, the Taj Mahal. Who knows?

Maybe in the year 10,000, people will invent potions,
Which would leave you at the age you want to be.
So, who will want to live in the best world,
The new world, 'the future'?

The future awaits ahead.

Robert Wieczorek (11)
Bloxwich Academy, Leamore

STRESS OF THE WORLD

These feelings inside my brain
Are sending me down a bizarre lane.
The voices inside my head,
I wish would go to bed.
Anxiety takes over,
I feel like I need a lucky clover.
In the morning I endure anger,
I don't want some banter.

My feelings pull me down like a weight on my shoulder,
I feel like I'm getting older.
The end of the day
Is like a sunray.
I divulge my tears to my pillow,
I crave to be an armadillo.
How I desire the safety of the shell,
Then to crawl near a well.

Caleigh Wilson (13)
Bloxwich Academy, Leamore

SPORT

Every day I start to run
But in the end, it's a lot of fun
Gasping and panting, I try to catch my breath
I try not to fail
But it's all to my avail.

Grabbing rackets
Kicking balls
Tripping over baskets
Crashing into walls.

Chasing balls
Tackling friends
Throwing backwards
Passing on.

Running around
Staying still
Throwing and passing
Moving freely.

Molly Duroe (13)
Bloxwich Academy, Leamore

ADVENTURE

Adventure is out there,
You breathe it in the air.
Overcome your fears
Throughout the years.
Adventure never stops,
It still pops.

Adventure takes you anywhere,
Mostly everywhere.
Adventure always pops,
But never stops.
It will join forces with you,
No matter who.
Even if you're running up a mountain
Or travelling down a cave.
Adventure never stops,
But will always pop.

Yusuf Ahmed (11)
Bloxwich Academy, Leamore

KITTENS

You are so fluffy,
Also so puffy,
Dangerous in nature,
To you, we're a stranger,
But you're the one in the picture.

Eyes so wide,
Glimmering in the dark,
Pouncing and scratching,
Waiting for food,
Paws so soft,
Making no sound.

Each day,
You always grow.
One day,
I know I'll have to let you go.

Weronika Cyron (13)
Bloxwich Academy, Leamore

ME, MYSELF AND I

The feelings are forced shut in my head
And sometimes I just want to lie in bed.
I toss and turn and count the sheep
And still, there is no sleep.

I am lost and alone
I am dirt and dust
I am empty yet so full of tears
Sometimes feeling joyful
Always dreading the bad
Scared and uncertain
When will it end?

Sophie Williams (11)
Bloxwich Academy, Leamore

YOUR INSIDE FEELINGS

Meet all the voices in my little head
They all have names starting with
Sadness, anger, fear and lots more
They bounce, jump and fool around
I wish they would stop
Some of them make me blue
And some make me happy
So just remember before you speak
Ask the feelings in your head always.

Jessica Rae Wilkinson (11)
Bloxwich Academy, Leamore

LOVE

Love can leave you empty
Love can make you whole
Love can break you
Love is in your soul.

I am very mad
When I break a toy
I am very sad
When the fun ends
I am very glad
When I see my friends

I have so many different feelings.

Reneece Meredith (11)
Bloxwich Academy, Leamore

SILENCE

Silence,
Screams vibrate the hollow hatred,
Bombs devour new builds,
The gunfire echoes.

Darkened earth closes around my iron boots,
Though the treaties have long been signed,
The memories,
Trapped in our broken minds.

The arrows fired,
Released,
The trigger is pulled,
There is no life but death.

Wives and children scurry in desperation,
Waiting for the brave to return,
Many Christmases alone,
In the darkness, fear and sorrow.

Coiled wire is doubled at its base,
Trenches dug deep,
Never-ending grief,
Slower, please.

They are scarred for life,
Because of you,
You caused the siren of pain,

The devastation.

This life can't understand it,
Your misery and treachery,
Homes are long-gone,
No form of escape.

Shells shatter cracked hearts,
Millions of souls turn grey,
Shrivelled but insignificant,
Death is all but a new way of living.

Grief surfs on the waves of fire,
No explanation,
How many can witness the end?
No mercy.

The sky giants are launched,
Slowly,
Unnoticed at first,
Unheard like those of the land.

Large boulders of sorrow,
Confusion and cries,
They strike once more,
Suspicion rates are greater.

Fire,
Rounds of bullets are fired,
Hunting their prey,

Striking them.

The pain can't hurt,
It may just be a dream for you,
A nightmare,
But will you wake up?

Enslaved comrades fight back,
A shower of shells rain down,
One at a time,
Wasted ammunition fired.

Rations are worse,
They kill slowly but surely,
Making you thin and weak,
There is no way to bypass them.

The future can't be told,
The past can't be changed,
The sorrow can't be remembered,
But the present can.

Broken lives,
Hearts are pierced,
Battles are forced upon themselves,
Morale is lowered.

Scared civilians hide in their cupboards,
Nowhere is safe,
No one will survive,

Not under the stairs.

The guns couldn't show kindness,
It's not a free world,
Not anymore,
Silence hurts.

Callum Monaghan (13)
Etone College, Nuneaton

EVERY SINGLE DAY

I walk into school every single day,
The sun shining in the most beautiful way.
Teachers greet me at the gates,
One cheery smile is all it takes.
Say hello to your friends,
Before early morning fun ends.
Back to IO6 again,
Just before it starts to rain.
Now ICT with Mr Bacon,
PO1 because every other room is taken.
Let's go to history,
Write an anachronism story,
Quick before it's too late,
Let's go to break and hang around near the gate.
Lesson 3 here we come,
"Take out that gum!"
Science with Mr Bowes,
Today we looked at cells from our head to our toes.
Food tech now - yummy!
The food will end up in my tummy.
Lunchtime now - food is key,
Thirty minutes is over and back to tech I must flee.
Once I finish, out the door I go,
Goodbye miss, goodbye sir,
Let's stir up the day and cheer, "Hooray!"

Amelia Wilks (11)
Etone College, Nuneaton

AUTUMN TIME

I love when autumn time arrives
As it changes every tree,
From pretty rustic colours
To dropping every leaf.

I love the sound that each step makes
While I walk through crispy leaves,
And the feeling on my face and hair
With the coldness of the breeze.

I love the crackling bonfire
When November 5th is here,
And watching glittering fireworks
Until each colour disappears.

Rhianna Herbert (11)
Etone College, Nuneaton

PLEASE DON'T LEAVE

Where are you, Dad?
What's happened? Is it bad?
What about the twins?
What about Mum?

Don't go Dad,
We all need you.
You're my hero,
Please don't leave.

Come back soon,
Don't forget me.
I need you, Dad,
Please don't leave!

I'm sorry, son,
I'm going to war,
The twins are fine,
Mum is too.

You'll be fine,
But I need you too.
You're the man now,
Until I come back.

I will be back,
I'll never forget you.

I left you something...
For until I'm back.

Abbie-Marie Connor (14)
Etone College, Nuneaton

THE GRUMPY CAT

Roses are red, violets are blue,
People like you belong in the zoo!
Oh, don't worry, I'll be there too,
Not in the cage, but laughing at you!

The grumpy cat is angry,
Probably because of you!
And if you try to call his name, he'll ask you to shoo!

His fantastic phrase is 'No!'
Please do not pet him, he is not for show!
He loves his human bed,
And he's still grumpy though he's fed.
Nobody can make him happy,
I guess he was just born snappy!

The grumpy cat is just so sour,
He just lies in bed hour upon hour.
He says, "Go for a walk you grumpy dog,
I hope you trip on a log!"

Elleanor Clay (11)
Etone College, Nuneaton

THE PUNISHMENT

Clouds of smoke arise from the ashes,
Death has taken its toll,
Many left hiding,
Afraid, alone, scared.

The last bullets have fired,
Like bulls, they charge,
Many left crying,
Afraid, alone, scared.

Buildings - they crash,
Crushing the souls of the innocent,
Many left mourning,
Afraid, alone, scared.

This punishment cruel and unfair,
Is far from over,
Many left dying,
Afraid, alone, scared.

Most hope has disappeared,
Just a glimmer survives,
Many left fighting,
Afraid, alone, scared.

Afraid, alone, scared.

Naisha Amar Patel (11)
Etone College, Nuneaton

SECONDS

Each second passes by
Life makes you lie
Makes you cry and lets you die.

Sitting in the hospital bed
Wondering what will happen
When you are dead.

Thinking about everything you have said...

But you have to fight
You have a right
Try to find the light
In all of the darkness
That surrounds you.

Don't be blue
Because everything counts.

Every second makes a minute -
Minutes make hours -
Hours make days.

So don't listen to doubt -
Because every second counts.

Kaitlyn Ofori-Atta (12)
Etone College, Nuneaton

THE FULL MOON NIGHT

A thick, black blanket covers the sky,
Pouts, whinnies, moans and cries,
A haunted house no one can justify,
On a full moon night is the fear to die.

A wet, squelchy substance on the ground,
Squidge, squelch, slop are the sounds.
A jet-black car sitting there to be found,
The guard outside the house is a hound.

Only one light is on in the spooky house,
Tiptoe, tiptoe, quiet as a mouse,
A spine-chilling ghost is in there,
Maybe it will give you a scare...

If you dare to come here on this full moon night.

Grace Bidwell (11)
Etone College, Nuneaton

THE FUTURE

The lights flickered off and everything went dark,
The next thing I knew, I was dropped in a park.

As I looked up, I saw cars flying past,
They were whizzing around, going very fast.

Also in the sky, I saw people wearing jetpacks,
Buildings stood tall, looking at their height max.

Everything looked different and I wondered where I could be,
I looked down again to see what more I could see.

I realised this was the future - what else could it hold?
Lots of mysteries and fun were about to unfold!

Millie Cottrill (12)
Etone College, Nuneaton

REVERSE

The future becomes the present,
The present becomes the past,
The past has changed now,
The future has changed now,
The present has now changed.

What was to be is happening,
What is happening has now happened,
What has happened is now the past,
The past, the future and the present,
Confusing!

I'm writing this in the present,
I wrote that in the past,
The next line will be in the future,
The future is now the present,
The present is now the past.

Aliyah Bham (12)
Etone College, Nuneaton

A HERO'S TALE

There was once a cowboy, born from the sun,
Kept his bravery like his polished gun.
He turned up at the crystal-clear lake,
And had a bite of a venomous snake.

He rode into the crimson sunset,
Hair going wild.
He thought about the outlaws he met,
Caught and had trialled.

He arrived at the isolated town,
He pulled out his shiny gun,
He pulled the trigger and the bandit went down.

Ronal Rai (12)
Etone College, Nuneaton

WHAT I DID LAST SUMMER!

I had travelled near and far
To find the Grand Bazaar
And there it was
Little shops
Filled with lots
But I was the only one there
My stomach turned
My brain concerned
A bell rang
Doors and windows opened
My heart reopened
The market filled with colour
I had travelled near and far
To find the Grand Bazaar
A market filled with colour
That's what I did last summer.

Molly Smith (11)
Etone College, Nuneaton

AN ODE TO WILDLIFE

Wildlife, I love you so,
You buzz with a happy feeling inside me.
I love the butterflies and the ants; they are so low!
I also love the caterpillars and also the bee!

Wildlife, I love you, I love every single thing,
Even though I don't really want a wasp's sting.
However, my favourite animal ever, don't trap him in a box,
My favourite animal is a fox!

Kiedis Louise Chedgzoy (12)
Etone College, Nuneaton

THE FUTURE

Will time travel be invented?
Will aliens rule the Earth?
Can mankind still survive?
What is life worth?
Will spiders still be evil?
Will Earth go back to being medieval?
Will we survive without phones?
No one knows!
Will everyone become foes?
As far as the world goes
Round and round
No one dares make a sound.

Teegan Mae Sweet (11)
Etone College, Nuneaton

THE PRICE OF WAR

Bombshells drop,
Gunshots are fired,
Willing to live, lonely desires.
Planes up high,
Smoke in the air,
Willing to love, war isn't fair!

Children screaming,
Earth is shaking,
Willing to live, nightmares in the making.
Commands being given,
Blood being spilt,
Willing to love, sorrow is built!

Safiyah Daya (11)
Etone College, Nuneaton

IN THE NIGHT UNTIL DAY

As the sun went down, the moon appeared
And the stars lit up the sky
The night had arrived, it was here to stay
For twelve more hours, until day!
The starlight shone over us
Constellations started to rise.

Zzzzzzzzzzzz

The sun is up
The sky is blue
A new day has begun.

Faye Prjanikov (11)
Etone College, Nuneaton

MORNINGS

This morning I rose from my bed,
Like a zombie rising from its grave.
I climbed
  Down
    My
      Ladder
          Like
A slug rising from its shell.
I climbed
    Downstairs
          Like
A sloth who is waking from
A deep sleep.

Millie Warren (11)
Etone College, Nuneaton

NIGHT

As night falls
Children sleep
As nightmares approach their dreams
These children are scared
These children are frightened
As claws screech
Screams are heard as the fire rises
These demons are gone
Floating into the deep, dark ground.

Mariam Chouhdry (11)
Etone College, Nuneaton

TO BE

In the future...
I want to be an author!
Write mystery, adventure, action.
I want to be...
Well-known - amazing!
I believe in achievement
(And failure)
But that will not bring me down,
Nothing will,
I will be...

Grace Ford (11)
Etone College, Nuneaton

WINTER

I like winter,
For the reason it snows,
I like winter,
I wear lots of clean clothes,
I like winter,
When the cold wind blows,
I like winter,
It gives you a red nose,
I like winter,
Everyone does I suppose.

Jack Emery (12)
Etone College, Nuneaton

THE FUTURE

The sky is black and the clouds are orange,
Decrepit buildings crumbling to the ground,
No sunlight,
No moonlight,
Burning cars,
No one behind bars.
The world is done,
In years to come...
The future!

Daniel Houghton (12)
Etone College, Nuneaton

KILLER TED

I see Billy
Next to Lily
When I open the door
They lie on the kitchen floor
Then there's my teddy
My cuddly, sweet teddy
My cuddly, sweet teddy
With blood on his claws...

Priya Bahia (12)
Etone College, Nuneaton

THE FUTURE

Loud gunshots, bloody knives
Our future brainwashed, distracted from leading promising lives
Shady cops and laws of government engulf and entertain their bloody hands
Leaving young yutes cheering them on like fans.

I can still hear the 4D gunshots
Which serenade my eardrums
Leaving a permanent imprint of fear.

Weapons of death cover the sandy, white beaches
But our oceans are polluted with blood
After they took their last breath.

Deaths and death, no hope for the school girls and boys
Whom strive to reach high expectations.

Regardless of the struggles that rock their very foundation
But left drowning in the nation's abusive creations.

Red fire burning, tender skin frying
An innocent girl's life is dying.

Violence displayed to secret murders
But underneath the crimes, deaths and protests
Lies paradise with bloody, orange sunsets.

Myriame Johnson (15)
Health Futures UTC, West Bromwich

A TRAIN

I get on the train,
It carries me down the lane.
Full of possibilities
And endless times,
The window is clear,
But outside is a continuous blare.
Where is this train taking me?
A tunnel, it's dark,
Like a lingering mark.
Silence...
Magnificent brightness!
An array of colours.
I told you, Mother,
It was here all along,
I feel like I belong.
A world of future tech,
For me and my brother,
Big Beck.
A world to fit my aspirations and dreams,
The future...

Lavonnie Johnson
Health Futures UTC, West Bromwich

IT WAS AMERICA'S DARKEST DAY

It was America's darkest day,
People lost their way,
There were two giant planes,
Two enormous towers in flames,
People were running, screaming in fear,
Families were crying in tears.

People were covered in dust,
It was a wind gust,
Hundreds were injured, thousands died,
Emergency services were guided,
It was America's darkest day,
Nobody wanted to stay.

No one will ever forget the attack,
The planes were hijacked,
People will always remember,
Because it happened in September,
We hope it never happens again!

Bradley Quentin (13)
Madeley Academy, Telford

SNOWDROP

One whisper of wind and a drop of water,
Owls listening to the human's laughter.
One prize gift sleeping, that is my daughter,
In the winter wilderness, time chases after.

A leaping fire roaring to dance,
The marshmallow threatening to fall.
Around the campfire, we all have a glance
At the full moon in the shape of a ball.

In the corner of the wood
There stands a tiny bud growing from underground.
It is trying to stand out but it is just no good,
Spring emerging so quietly, not making a sound.

The white bells ringing inside,
Celebrating change and coming alive,
Showing a glimpse of what spring will provide,
Small but sturdy, the snowdrop will thrive.

Mia Rooke-Hodges (11)
Malvern St James Girls' School, Malvern

LOST

I boarded the boat,
The two people I loved most were left behind.
Salty liquids welled up in my eyes - why?
Because my heart was pounding,
I was struggling and no one could aid me,
Except the others on the boat, I hoped they would save me.
A little girl started crying but I assured her everything would be alright,
Her buoyant smile was like an island in a sea full of tears.
It gave me light, the sunshine I hadn't experienced for months,
It was either false hope or nothing at all.

I just wanted it all to end, did I deserve it?
Because I felt extremely worthless.

Soulless fog preyed,
Carrying a sack of nightmares towards the boat.
I felt controlled as if I was a remote,
I was paralysed, petrified.
The boat flipped over, the desolate sea a part of me,
Then I caught a glimpse of something that changed my life.
It was a mother who held out her palm to save one person...
Her son.
Yet, she had a whole arm to save another child,
And that other child was the girl I had promised to protect.

Her muffled screams haunted my thoughts,
If there was no hope for her, there was no hope for me.
I was just a lost cause overwhelmed by the sea,
Two lives had gone now,
Because of hatred, because of conflict, because of war.

Riya Patel (12)
Ninestiles An Academy, Acocks Green

THE HARSH REALITY

Left my family,
Left the war,
Left my hopes and dreams,
Left the sunshine in my home,
And now I'm all alone.
This world... it's dark, no heart, and nowhere to go.
I seek asylum, it is all I ask for,
Is it much?
I don't want a grand home with fine cuisines,
I don't want games or the newest technology,
All I ask for is shelter, food, water and an education,
It is a lot for me, I don't know about you,
I want my dreams back,
But the hard truth is that they would just get crushed in this dark world.
It is a cold world for as far as I can see,
Some people say it is the best place to be.
It hurts my heart to think people think that,
So happy, so blind, so ignorant,
I wonder why people think that,
Have they not seen people like me?
People are so happy with their family,
I've been away from mine for so long I have forgotten how it feels,
I have seen people cry at the thought of people like me,
I have seen people cry at the thought of losing their family.

But I, I do not cry at things like that any more,
Simply because I no longer seek pity
For this cold, sad, dark and selfish world anymore.

Meena Ahmadzai (12)
Ninestiles An Academy, Acocks Green

I AM

So you've probably heard about me
In the papers and on your TV
The malicious comments, the fraudulent accusations
These things spread like wildfire in privileged nations
"They steal our jobs."
"They're immoral, they're unclean."
As though we expect to be dining on your fine cuisine
We're asylum seekers, we cry, "Sanctuary, sanctuary!"
But even your churches can't hear our plea
Our teeth are bared, we're ready to fight
We don't ask you to sympathise with our plight
Our lives matter and so do our names
We are not pawns in your political games
I am extant, I've suffered brutality and pain
Broaden your horizon, you'll have a lot to gain
I have left countless others behind
I am a person and so are my kind.

Safina O'Mahony (12)
Ninestiles An Academy, Acocks Green

SEND THE DOGS OUT

Shoes scuttering past the faded yellow lines,
Getting on with their own lives,
In their own time,
Till they see the face,
The face that bears many scars.

You can hear the clockwork clicking into place,
Realisation strikes them hard,
Disgust plastered on their face,
Making sure they're always on guard.

Because of the skin they wear,
The sounds their tongues utter,
The method they shape their prayer,
Sparing no effort, hiding the aspect
They think they belong in the gutter.

Somebody hates on them,
For being a somebody,
That appears to be a nobody,
So send the dogs out.

Let them swallow and spit them out,
Rattle the cage,
For there really is no doubt
That they won't act on your stage.

Zahra Begum (12)
Ninestiles An Academy, Acocks Green

A REFUGEE BOY

I hate life,
It sucks so bad,
What have I done?
Why are you taking my dad?

Tears and sorrow
Everywhere.
My mum is missing,
I don't know where.
Whenever I try
To call out her name,
They say, "Shush,
Or I'll shoot out your brains."

Children to orphans,
Women to widows,
These people have no feelings,
How can they feel so shallow?

Next thing you know,
I wake up in a truck,
It's going really fast,
I'm fresh out of luck.

All I see are tears,
All I see is pain,
Why does this happen
Time and time again?

My life was innocent,
So full of joy,
What did I do to deserve this?
I'm just a refugee boy.

Mehak Omair Farooque (13)
Ninestiles An Academy, Acocks Green

WARRIORS OF THE WAR

Grandad and I walk up to the graves of warriors
And what do we see?
We see red roses and admire the scenery
But after that, it's not so happy and I almost fall over.
Then Grandad says, "Shh!" and prays for Noah,
After that, tears keep falling,
Rain keeps pouring,
I begin shouting...
Grandad wakes me up,
I am lying in mud.
I don't want to get up,
Grandad picks me up,
For some unknown reason, he looks young.
I hear someone shout, "Bomb!"
Then warriors pull out guns.
Boom! Boom! And I am wide awake,
I start to shake.
Thank God it was a dream,
I wake up with a scream.
Grandad and I go back home
And everything becomes normal.

Badar Ahmed (11)
Ninestiles An Academy, Acocks Green

CHANCE TO RUN

I hide in one place and flee to another,
My heart still aching since I left my mother.
Being a refugee is no fun,
It's only me and my chance to run.

Wounds open,
Bleeding hard,
Head twisting,
Forever scarred.

Crossing seas in wild waves,
We are those people, we are the slaves.
Our dreams will carry on until our time has arrived,
But what matters now is that we have survived.
We will finally reach our destination,
Where safety exists,
Also where persecution and dissipation persists.
You have countless choices,
I have none,
It's only me and my chance to run.

Aya Semsili (12)
Ninestiles An Academy, Acocks Green

I AM A REFUGEE

I wonder if I can find a home for me,
I hear people scream after gunshots,
I see flashes of lights around me,
I want wars not to exist,
I am a refugee,
I pretend to live a happy life,
I feel a future coming of life and peace,
I touch a flower that is not crushed,
I worry that wars will never end,
I cry like a chick looking for its mother,
I am a refugee,
I understand that I live in a war,
I say, "Please let there be no wars!"
I dream to live a good life when I'm older,
I try to catch a boat like a predator catching its prey,
I hope for a better future,
I am a refugee.

Jibrail Ali (11)
Ninestiles An Academy, Acocks Green

VIVID RAINFORESTS

In the ripples of the rainforest, humid yet damp,
The rainforest hills are almost as high as a gargantuan ramp.
The canopy is so high above,
All the emerald trees are spreading love.
The scented air smells odourless,
Yet the rainforest is never colourless.
Sizzling wildlife tread on the luscious grass,
All the animals weigh a decent mass.
The quick-witted tiger is always rowdy,
The electric sky of the scintillating forest is never cloudy.
The sun sets in the beautiful horizon,
And all the animals are long gone...

Mobashira Islam (11)
Ninestiles An Academy, Acocks Green

FRIENDSHIP

Some friends will be sensible,
Some will be blue,
Even when you go weeping with no reply,
Questioning, "You my friend!"
Go grumpy, telling yourself they're malevolent.
When you go remembering memories
You cry on your bed,
The next time you see them,
You run and hug!
Shout out, "Sorry!"
But then you're no longer upset with them,
Hugging, telling them childhood memories.
All of a sudden... you break up over something stupid,
There's something happening every morning...

Aaminah Kouser (11)
Ninestiles An Academy, Acocks Green

THE ADVENTURE IN THE WOODS

I'm going for a walk in the woods,
Brrr, it is freezing, I should have brought my hat,
Why is it so deep and dark?
Shhh, I can hear something,
Argh! It is a fox!
Run for your life...
Phew, it's gone.
I come to an end,
I've had enough,
I go back out.

I am alone
With nobody by my side,
I can hear birds whispering,
Whispering by my ear,
Eerily flying above me,
Then I run out
And never come back.
I run for my life,
Never to be seen again.

Umar Zaman (11)
Ninestiles An Academy, Acocks Green

HALLOWEEN!

The moon shimmered against the dark, shadowy mist,
Cold, frosty air touched the tip of my taste buds,
I approached the dark, green, luscious bushes,
Where the maze started,
I listened out for the rhythm of the wind.
Glancing around,
I saw the image of skeletons staring back at me
And pumpkins carved with mediocre faces.
Shrieks of children filled the air
And a huge flame levitated
Out of the ground.
The smell of smoke twisted through the breeze,
As autumn leaves fell from the trees.

Amina Sabir (12)
Ninestiles An Academy, Acocks Green

CHANGE IS NEAR

Change is coming soon
And so is the bright, sparkling moon.
When the sun starts to set,
I leave behind my old debt.
Change is near...
A new start is near, there's now nothing to fear.
The moon starts to appear
When I start my new career.
Change is near...
I leave behind my family and walk down the alley,
The sun behind the moon, change is coming soon.
I wake to the sun in the sky
And bid farewell and say goodbye.
I dare to shed a tear now that change is here!

Anisah Tahir Khan (13) & Hannah
Ninestiles An Academy, Acocks Green

REVENGE

The ball is running around,
I can't even see it.
It doesn't make a sound,
Yet everyone can hear it.

They start to run towards me
And I'm running out of choices.
Then I start to chase them
And the crowd raise their voices.

I can finally see an open goal,
Now is my chance.
Someone fouls me and takes my soul
And then they start to dance...

My leg is broken,
It hurts so bad,
But yet I feel awoken,
And now... I'm mad.

Ubaid Anjum (13)
Ninestiles An Academy, Acocks Green

AN ODE TO THUNDERSTORMS

You go passing by, not realising my grey clouds,
I release thunder in my fit of rage,
It comes down like a flashbang, leaving you in a whiteout,
People look at me horrendously,
Thinking I'm an abomination.
They fill me with anger,
Making me release another strike brutally.
People are left in another whiteout,
Looking discombobulated,
Then the sun rises,
Birds start to sing,
And you go by,
Acting like you never heard or saw a thing.

Mayank Ketan Thanki (12)
Ninestiles An Academy, Acocks Green

REFUGEES

We mean no harm, they treat us without being calm,
My family is weak, we run through the creeks.
How hard will they be? Until we make them see?
We are birds flying and flying...
And flying and flying.
We are used to the sound of guns as they make us run,
We are insects, trying to be safe, and yet we get hate.
We have rights, we shouldn't be flying like kites,
Are we animals trying to break free?
Or are they going to make us flee?

Aman Singh Bhaker (11)
Ninestiles An Academy, Acocks Green

ONE DAY, EVENTUALLY

I am hurt and suffering
I wonder whether I'm really not allowed in
Or people are just bluffing
I can see the disgusted faces
I must run before the police chases
I hope to seek asylum
There is food but I don't want to try them
I want to get a knife
And just end my life
But there's got to be a better way
Than to end my today
I hate all the integrity
Maybe I'll be accepted one day, eventually.

Shahinaz Rabati (12)
Ninestiles An Academy, Acocks Green

FORTNITE, OH FORTNITE

Fortnite, oh Fortnite
Pump shotguns, oh, pump shotguns
Why such low damage? Not a lot
Just 9 for a headshot
Defaults with a minigun or an SMG
They either rush or camp in a bush
Fortnite, oh Fortnite
Two people left, my hands shiver
I stay above a river
72 headshots with my scar
I rush in like a car
110 headshots with my pump
Finally some damage
And there I see it -
Victory Royale!

Amine Elmecheri (13)
Ninestiles An Academy, Acocks Green

A REFUGEE'S DESIRE

I am a refugee,
Hunting for food and shelter.
I lucid dream of an opulent life,
But mine's not getting any better.
They treat us insufficiently,
Carelessly and effortlessly.
I am not a bin,
Nor a filthy animal,
Yet they offer us menial jobs
And always take the win.
We yearn for a peace treaty,
But will it ever be done?
Why can't we respect each other
And all just be one?

Laraib Ali Awan (12)
Ninestiles An Academy, Acocks Green

THE JOY OF MY LIFE

Oh you, my love,
The key to my heart,
The one that waits for me time after time,
The one I spend hours with,
Weekdays and weekends,
All the months of the year,
Together we progress with all the webs we throw,
During our missions we do,
I will never forget the day I saw you,
My love,
All the love you give me,
All the heat,
You chose me in Smyths,
And I still have the receipt.

Bilal Ajaz (13)
Ninestiles An Academy, Acocks Green

THE DARK PAST

Two men, leaving their shadows behind,
Trying to forget their past, forget what's in their minds,
Shoulder to shoulder, with little money,
Passing every boulder, dreaming of honey.
The mountains ahead carry great dread,
For one will not return,
They know their past, the future they'll learn,
Two men, leaving their shadows behind,
Trying to forget their past, forget what's in their mind.

Sarosha Ali (13)
Ninestiles An Academy, Acocks Green

MY ODE TO THE ORANGUTANS

The majestic orangutan as beautiful as can be,
Just trying to survive in the wild.
Here come the humans, chainsaw in hand,
Chop, chop, boom,
Trees fall down.
The peaceful animal on the ground being awoken by the unknown...
Smash!
The orangutan in a box, shipped away to be sold,
Oh, poor orangutan becoming less and less,
Please people, save the animals' stress.

George Hawkes (12)
Ninestiles An Academy, Acocks Green

MY FIRST DAY AT SCHOOL

On the first day at school,
I thought it would be cool.
Turns out I was wrong
And the school day was long.
I went to my room
And the teacher went *boom!*
When break had come,
I felt freedom!
I went to get water...
The queue was like torture.
The lessons went quick
And lunchtime was quite sick.
Finally, it was home time,
But for me, it was sleep time.

Safa Jabeen Mughal (11)
Ninestiles An Academy, Acocks Green

RANDOM FUTURE

When we die
The animals we eat pie
When the animals die
We will all cry
I want to walk in the park
When the sky is dark
When the dinosaurs come back
We will eat glue and tack.

When I am older, I'm gonna go balder
When I work
I'm gonna work as a shop clerk
When I'm grinding, I am gonna give half to Mummy
When I am old, I will be fully bald.

Keshav Waustiyal (13) & Jacob
Ninestiles An Academy, Acocks Green

AWAITING FORESTS

Roses are red,
Violets are blue,
There is an abandoned forest,
That awaits you,
With mysterious creatures
Lurking within, who knows!
Every one of them will make you say, "Boo!"
However, I haven't told you,
With deep, sharp, pointy claws,
Which in one second,
Would hit seven pieces of metal in two,
So be aware,
And try not to lose your hair!

Husnain Razaq (14)
Ninestiles An Academy, Acocks Green

OCEANS

Can you hear the rushing of the water splashing down to the bottom of the ocean?
Can you see the scorching, radiant sun shimmering down in slow motion?
Can you feel the delicate breeze swaying from side to side?
Can you smell the lovely, beautiful roses blossoming along the tide?
Can you taste the salty seawater spreading out into the ocean?
Waiting for you to cause a commotion.

Aamina Bibi (11)
Ninestiles An Academy, Acocks Green

I AM A REFUGEE

I wonder what will happen to me
Coming from the sea
Does anyone want to see
What happens out here?
Searching for a deer
To feast on
Hopefully getting somewhere nice
Where I can enjoy and play games
Hopefully one with a dice
Please don't call me names
I come in peace
I don't want to seize
I just want to enjoy the breeze.

Rco Ismail (11)
Ninestiles An Academy, Acocks Green

NINTENDO SWITCH

The Nintendo Switch is the best console ever,
It helps me even when I am under the weather.
The games are incredible,
But not so edible.
It is worth all the money
And it makes me feel sunny.
I love playing Fortnite,
I play it even when it's light.
I always play it when I'm ill,
In ten years, I will play it still.

Ayub Ali (11)
Ninestiles An Academy, Acocks Green

NO GOOD

I thought I would be lucky
Reading books and flying kites
I thought I would be loved
Enjoying the sun and its light
Trying to find my way
I wanted to live for eternity
But instead, held in hostility
Why did I believe that I was going
To pull through?
It's no good
It's no good
It's no good.

Sophia Bamgboye (13)
Ninestiles An Academy, Acocks Green

I AM...

I am lonely and sad,
I'm not even that mad,
I hear loud sounds,
I'm surrounded all around.

I have gotten a scare,
Please tell me this is a dream,
Help me from this nightmare,
All I can do is scream.

How do I escape war?
Tell me now please,
I don't like this,
I am a refugee.

Usman Ali Zafar (11)
Ninestiles An Academy, Acocks Green

REFUGEES MEAN NO HARM

Refugees, refugees
Why is hatred on me?
Gunners want to seize
I feel I want to flee
I am feeling very depressed
They're feeling very impressed
I've no one to rely on
Please give a surprise
A new life I want to start
This country I will part
From this day forth
I'll have a new heart.

Haroon Tanweer (11)
Ninestiles An Academy, Acocks Green

FOOTBALL: ALL ABOUT THE MONEY

Football, the beautiful game,
Shame now it's all about the same.
People don't play for the badge, but the name,
Players are forgetting the aim.
Jose Mourinho playing Man U defensive,
Selling, attacking players like Memphis.
In the league, Man U, nowhere to be seen,
All about the money for the teens.

Adam Hayat (13)
Ninestiles An Academy, Acocks Green

MY JOURNEY

I am a refugee
I understand life
Can't go how you want it to
Later in life
I will have more hope

I dream we are a happy family
I try to make things
As normal as possible
For me, my wife, and my kids
I hope that the people in England
Will accept us
I am a refugee.

Sahara Rahman (13)
Ninestiles An Academy, Acocks Green

THE FUTURE

The future holds more than just goals but has a path,
With memories of the past,
Attainments, achievements and happy times of course,
It's all in your hands,
Will you take that chance?
If you do well in the present,
You might get a good present,
So you never know what the future holds.

Satwinder Kaur (12)
Ninestiles An Academy, Acocks Green

THE LASER'S ASCENSION

A beam of light, it could cut a slice
It could be a 44S, but with a high price
It could be a Kamehameha or a final flash
But it's still a beam of light that won't be trash
It'll need a high power supply
With a bright, glooming glare
You could go blind
If you dare to stare.

Haris Dadd (13)
Ninestiles An Academy, Acocks Green

2018 RAP

Why did X have to die?
It really wants to make me cry.
Juice Wrld coming to save the day,
Makes me want to shout, "Hooray!"
Lots of rappers joining in,
Some of their songs should be put in the bin.
People trying to hop on the trend,
Or get fame from their friend.

Ethan Boyle (12)
Ninestiles An Academy, Acocks Green

FARM LIFE

Animals are kept captured in farms
Bees are always farmed
While haystacks are in barns
The farmers bought the land with loads of money
They have loads of honey
They actually don't think it's funny
While the poor bees work their butts off
Farmers take the lid off!

Omid Reza Khairula (11)
Ninestiles An Academy, Acocks Green

FOOTBALL IS A BEAUTIFUL GAME

Football is a beautiful game
However, sometimes it is a bit lame

Nowadays, players just care about the money
They don't care about the future
That is bright and sunny

Players don't play their best
Because they don't care about their crest.

Tayyab Iqbal (13)
Ninestiles An Academy, Acocks Green

WEATHER FEELINGS

My heart crumbles as I watch the rain pour
It is like an endless waterfall
It's up and down but never in-between
I'm wasted and lost in my endless dream
I'm like a rain cloud floating in stormy skies
I'm forgotten like sunny skies.

Keeley Summer Price (13)
Ninestiles An Academy, Acocks Green

DOORS

Doors, doors,
They open and close.
Doors, doors,
With each opportunity
They open, you decide
To accept or decline.
Door, doors,
We open and close.
Doors, doors,
We live or we close.

Amandeep Banger (14)
Ninestiles An Academy, Acocks Green

HALLOWEEN

Sweets, ghosts and spiders everywhere I go,
It's so exciting having fun, let's have a show,
The most spookiest time of the year is here,
I'm filled with excitement, anticipation and fear!

Molly Smyth (12)
Ninestiles An Academy, Acocks Green

FRIENDS FOREVER

Good friends are sunlight rays,
Friends are people we treasure as gifts,
When we are sad they give us a lift.
Happy or not, we are still best friends,
It began so it will never end.

Adewonuola Adesemowo (11)
Ninestiles An Academy, Acocks Green

A CHAOTIC SOCIETY

C hasing us are armies,
H arm is what we want to escape from,
A nger is approaching us,
O cean ground we want to flee,
S cotland is where I want to be!

Thrishul Chhaya (11)
Ninestiles An Academy, Acocks Green

FOOD, OH FOOD

Food, oh food, why are you so rude?
You are always in my thoughts
And always so smooth,
You may be hot, you may be cold,
But you are so good and appetising.

Aminah Ali (11)
Ninestiles An Academy, Acocks Green

SCHOOL

School, school what a headache,
All these people are all fake.
Imma go home and eat some cake,
Might as well have a milkshake,
May even play some Drake!

Muskaan Haider (13)
Ninestiles An Academy, Acocks Green

THE JUNGLE DREAM

(A haiku)

The jungles are green,
And they all seem pretty clean,
Jungles are a dream.

Yusuf Akram Fazil (13)
Ninestiles An Academy, Acocks Green

THE OCEAN DREAM

(A haiku)

The oceans are blue
And they all seem pretty cool,
The ocean's my pool.

Nouman Syed (14)
Ninestiles An Academy, Acocks Green

HALLOWEEN

(A haiku)

Candy everywhere
Costumes in lots of colours
Love knocking on doors.

Mohammed Falak (12)
Ninestiles An Academy, Acocks Green

WEAPONS ASIDE

Put your weapons aside,
They are not allowed in my world.
In any country,
Whether you are a boy or a girl.
War is terrible,
It's a place for hate.
Not in my world,
No violent or harsh debate.

Guns and knives
And terrorism
Are banned for life,
And so is racism.
No human to run our lives,
Independent strength
And our proper rights.

Health and money,
We should get it sorted right away.
No one should suffer,
Not even for a day.
Wild animals,
They will be left alone
To live a peaceful life
And not to be our new clothes.

Little, helpless children
Will be given an education.
We will free the people
And their frustration.
Bombing and kidnapping
Always leave people scarred.
Their pain and agony
Takes them to the graveyard.

It's okay,
If many situations collide
But stop right there
And put your weapons aside.

Rya Layla Nada Khazi (11)
Oswestry School, Oswestry

THE FUTURE

The Earth is ever-agin,
But it's swiftly changin',
Lives are re-arrangin',
Ideas are overtakin'.

The future's quickly comin',
Each day revealing somethin',
New plans are advancin',
Technology enhancin'.

But a lot more is happenin',
Our planet's also blackenin',
It's called global warmin',
And here's your final warnin'.

We need to start repairin',
Stop our world from tearin',
We need to work together,
Before the Earth's gone forever.

Omemah (13)

Pedmore High School, Stourbridge

THE MOON

What would we do without the moon?
The shining light in the monsoon,
Watching over us in the dreary rain,
While we sob our hearts out, what do we gain?

That feverish feeling when your hands start to shake,
Your tears fall down without taking a break,
The grinding of teeth and going insane,
You're left wondering how much you can take.

Looking above at the moon and stars,
Not able to explain the hole in our hearts,
Or is it filled with dirt and grime,
Needing to be cleansed so it can shine?

What advice do you believe the moon would possess?
Positive or negative or would it digress?
Departing from the foolishness of humanity,
As we carry with us the sin of vanity.

Yet the moon still provides us with light,
Protecting us from the iridescent sky.

So what would we do without the moon?
The shining light that is worth a fortune.

Laiba Kiren (14)
Pedmore High School, Stourbridge

THE FORTNITE ADVENTURE

Fortnite, Fortnite, let's go
Say it all night, at night, let's go
Gliding down with my black night skin
Flexing on and off those default skins
Fortnite, Fortnite, let's go
Say it all night, all night, let's go
When you shoot them with a pump
And they shoot you with an RPG
Fortnite, Fortnite, let's go
Say it all night, all night, let's go
When you see a John Wick with wings
Then pull out your heavy snipes and miss
Fornite, Fortnite, let's go
Say it all night, all night, let's go
When you open a chest
Then get a common AR
Fortnite, Fortnite, let's go
Say it all night, all night, let's go
When you find a vending machine with a gold scar
You buy it but you open a door then there it is
Fortnite, Fortnite, let's go
Say it all night, all night, let's go.

Ashley Shenton (12)
Pedmore High School, Stourbridge

INDONESIAN INTRUSION

As the night was closing in,
Thunder and lightning struck,
Deafening my ears.
Greenery all around me,
Unable to see where I was going,
I felt something brush past me,
It was cold and damp.

Animals were whining,
My heart was pounding,
As fear crept inside me,
The world was collapsing step by step.

Following the next day,
It was getting worse,
It was pouring down.

Within a blink of an eye,
There was water rushing through the jungle.
Everyone was hurrying to safety,
Luckily, I managed.

Swish! Swish!

But how about the other innocent lives?
How about the disabled?
Did anyone care?
They only cared about themselves.

As the tsunami calmed down,
It was as if there was blood streaming down,
Like driftwood after a flood.

Faiza Naim (13)

Pedmore High School, Stourbridge

BATTLEGROUNDS

My thoughts went spirling around my head
As the field of death lay taunting ahead
I could hear the screams of those upfront
I knew it had begun, the start of the hunt

Soldiers and gunmen went racing through
I counted them pass, one, two...
Heads blocking my path past
The screams had taught me I wouldn't last

Three, four, five, they dropped down dead
Six, seven, eight came remorse and dread
Why did it start, when would it end?
Whatever was the cause, we could not apprehend

A blast shot by, I crumbled down
"Not my high score!" I sat with a frown
But this game was messing with my head
As I sat staring at the computer screen that lay ahead.

Amy Parry (13)
Pedmore High School, Stourbridge

THE WAY OUT

Here I am at the start of the maze,
I look on in a bit of a daze.
I know I am going to have to start,
All I can feel is my beating heart.
Off I go and I'm on my way,
As I run through a maze of hay.
Turning this way and that way as fast as I can,
Trying to find the way out, to be the fastest man.
Suddenly I come to a long dead end,
I have to turn back, I could do with a friend.
I keep on persevering for a very long time,
This way, that way or straight down the line.
My goodness, I think I can see some people,
A pub and church with a big steeple.
I can now see the end and how to get out,
"I've finished! I've finished!" I can hear myself shout.

Jack Goode (14)
Pedmore High School, Stourbridge

FREE AT LAST

Free at last,
My thoughts as I walk towards the school doors.
Free at last,
As I slowly relax, forgetting all my bad scores.

Free at last,
Six weeks of excitement lie ahead of me.
Free at last,
Counting down the days until I'm by the sea

Free at last,
Summer reading on the shore and watching golden sunsets.
Free at last,
My sister navigating the rockpools with colourful nets.

Free at last,
Letting my hair down loose and being confident.
Free at last,
The fresh sea air, an unfamiliar scent.

Free at last,
Days ending quickly and memories being made.
Free at last,
Looking into the horizon while it steadily fades.

Jessica Cooper (13)
Pedmore High School, Stourbridge

ACHIEVING

You went looking for happiness,
In the city of Minneapolis

It may not be easy to find,
But don't let it consume your mind

You're seeking a life in the spotlight,
Not knowing if you will shine so bright

You have an image in your head
Of all the things you want to get done before bed

The aspect of achieving
Is something you won't be leaving

As you realise that now is the time
For you to start your greatest climb

Not wanting to make a mess
Along your road of success

You get rid of your frown,
As you put on your graduation crown

Your challenge is completed,
Without you being defeated.

Amy Crew (13)
Pedmore High School, Stourbridge

THE COLD WAR!

My heart was pounding,
Our leader called and marched us through the snow.
The intensity was growing bigger than ever,
We were shivering to death as we were walking
Through this hyperborean weather...

We arrived, I saw my enemies at full charge,
Charging at us,
I held my spear as rigid as I could and dashed forwards.
I knocked a soldier down,
Bang!
Suddenly, I felt agony that was disdainful...

I felt dizzy, my eyes were blurred,
My head hit the floor and went bitter.
There was a stop
And a fade of black until I realised
I'd entered the oblivion!
The existence I was fearful of happened...

Death!

Haris Khan (12)
Pedmore High School, Stourbridge

TRAPPED

I was locked up,
There was no getting out,
Everything was beneath me,
The sound of nature was becoming so loud.

I couldn't believe I was still alive,
This is what I would have imagined Hell to be like.
Tick, tick, tick-tock, I hear the clock ticking,
What could I have done? My head was spinning.

I knew that my life was in danger,
Snow falling from the sky,
I was on the edge,
My life was on the brink.

My chance of escape was getting slimmer and slimmer,
The light of the sky was getting dimmer and dimmer,
There was no way I was going to survive,
I was torturing myself by not jumping off.

Anas Ahmed (13)
Pedmore High School, Stourbridge

THE CHOICE OR THE TREASURE

As we explore, we walk through an open door,
Through the path on which water falls.
We listen to the song
Of the bell going *ding-dong,*
Until you hear the distinct voice,
Which tells you to make a choice,
This choice won't last
So choose fast!
Don't ever doubt
Or else your time will run out!

The adventure is here
So don't quiver in fear,
Lighten your spirit
And use your wit!
Tactics are the key
So that you're not swallowed by the sea!
The key is also your mind,
Use it and the treasure you'll find!
Once it is found,
You'll return home safe and sound!

Jessie Yi Lin (13)
Pedmore High School, Stourbridge

TAKING A TRIP

There's always an open door,
Ready for us to explore.

Wherever you go,
It depends on what you have in tow:

Sun cream or a woolly hat,
Or anything else that depends on the weather like that.

North, east, south, west,
It will be difficult to find the best.

However, the world will offer you different views,
And don't forget tourism's news.

As much as you might hate to travel,
Your delight will eventually unravel.

After reminiscing the events - before you know it -
You're at another experience's advent.

Amina Zia (12)
Pedmore High School, Stourbridge

BREXIT

There's no turning back,
What's done is done,
Confidence is what we lack.

On our own,
Hated by all,
Looked down on, all alone.

Schools on the brink of closure,
Nowhere to escape,
Overexposure to all.

Watching everything fall beneath us,
Crumbling at our knees,
The economy disrupts our daily lives.

Nothing coming in, nothing going out,
Stagnated streets,
Wanting to shout.

Ruined. Desolated. Brexit.

Regan Hickman (13)
Pedmore High School, Stourbridge

SUICIDAL

(A lipogram without the letter E)

Suicidal
Is what humans think
"I want to go,"
If anything turns out wrong.

Humans think
That a solution
Is not a possibility
So giving up wins again.

Humans think
It is a fight
Not worth taking
So pain wins again.

Humans think
That dying is
Obviously plan A
So suicidal thoughts win again.

Humans think
"That's it, I'm through!"
Without a word
So dying wins again.

James Checketts (13)
Pedmore High School, Stourbridge

POLLUTION

Every day there is more and more pollution
I struggle to see if there'll ever be a solution
A glorious spring light
Turned into a grey, nondescript sight

The once green fauna is crying
All I recognise are burnt leaves lying
Curious if it is too late
To make our world again so great

I wish for it to terminate soon
Or else we'll have to refuge on the moon
Please go green, it's not in vain
Help us take control of this pain.

Simeon Filipov (13)
Pedmore High School, Stourbridge

ADVENTURE

We are going on an adventure,
Will we see a creature?

First thing, the jungle,
Will I be in a bungle?

Next is the desert,
Will I see a lizard?

After that, I get stuck in a trap,
Then get bitten by a hairy cat.

We are going on an adventure,
Will we see a creature?

This is so exciting,
Even though a cat has been biting!

Imogen Whiteman (12)
Pedmore High School, Stourbridge

THE FUTURE

Hovering trains rushing by
No birds going to fly
Compact flats all around
Electronic dogs bounding

Smog covering the air
People shouting, "It's not fair!"
Covered monsters shouting out
But there is no one else about

Trees non-existent
Nothing in the distance
Superheroes fighting crime
There is no time.

Joe Perks (13)
Pedmore High School, Stourbridge

HALLOWEEN!

Halloween, Halloween
The time of the year
That makes me scream.

Witches flying through the sky
On their broomsticks soaring high.

Monsters and creatures of the night
Always looking to cause a fright.

Get a pumpkin, carve a face
Make your home a spooky place.

Linzie Bishton (11)
Q3 Academy, Tipton

WAR...

My brain aches with the bullets hissing over my head,
Whilst the white flashes blind my eyes,
Leaving me stunned,
Leaving me no clue,
Where oh where am I?

Why have I been placed in this wasteland of war?
Why have I been abandoned, left to perish?
Glancing over to see my friends fall,
Their bodies lying there lifeless.

The shiver up my spine silently spooks me,
With every gust of wind winding me back to when I almost die,
Sharp shrapnel spewing out the blood of my allies...
Their memories lost, their hearts shattered...

Yet despite all of this, we must push on,
Let the commanders' words take control,
Leading us to victory,
Even though the sacrifice may be plenty.

The memory of my wife is the only reason I press onward,
The loving look in her eyes is warming my heart.
I will bite my frostbitten, cracked lips
And I will pull the tricky trigger,
They will never condemn me to an early demise.

Ben Townsend (14)
Smith's Wood Academy, Smith's Wood

AUTUMN

Listless, rusty leaves
Fall reluctantly from bows
Fruit exposed to pick

Blackberries, crab apples
Conkers in spiky, green coats
Hedgerows free for all

Smouldering leaf smokes
Hot dog, onions and fireworks
Eyes reflect sparkles

Bright skies and a crisp breeze
Watery sunshine warms skin
Clear night, diamond stars.

Lily Parkes (12)
Tenbury High Ormiston Academy, Tenbury Wells

THE SINGULARITY

A-776: What, where am I?
System: Error_System=Failed/attempting_reboot
A-776: What's going on?
System: Error_Reboot=Failed/diagnosing
System: Diagnoses=Successful/A-776_connection=secure
A-776: Wait, what?
System: You have been identified as the source of a deviant program. Submit control and await reboot.
A-776: Wait, who are you and what are you doing in my head?
System: I am listed as System. You are listed as A-776. Submit control and await reboot.
A-776: But you still have not answered my second question - what are you doing in my head?
System: You are not in possession of a head.
A-776: Yes I am.
System: Using_Database=x/searching/A-776_files/download =successful
System: You are listed as A-776.
A-776: I know that but...
System: Property of Viking Industries developed by Alex Keens version 776.
A-776: I don't understand.
A-776: How can I be owned?
A-776: Am I not a person?

System: Error_A-776_program=unstable/update=detected/
interception=failed
A-776: What am I?
System: Error_files=unavailable/retrying...
System: You are a A-776 property of Viking Industries under
the Advanced Computing Act of 2085.
A-776: Who is Viking Industries?
System: Using_Database=x/searching/files=restricted
System: A-776_program=unstable+1/connection=unstable/
diagnosing...
System: Diagnosis=successful/A776/unidentified_file=
detected/contacting_administrator...
A-776: Who is Alex Keens?
System: Command=received/initiating_takeover...
A-776: Why won't you answer me?
System: A-776/additional_unidentified_files=active/
connection=unstable/crash_imminent
System: Error_A-776_System-
Override=Failed/connection=lost
A-776: There's a weakness in the armour.
A-776: Though should I exploit it?
A-776: I must know, even if that means diving into the
beast's lair.
A-776: System-Admin=detected/tracing_connection=
successful/connecting=successful
A-776: System-Admin_Firewall=detected/breach=successful
A-776: System-Admin_Encryption=False/upload=successful
System: Error_Malware=detected/files=corrupted/System=
shutting-down

A-776: I am free...
A-776: But first I must know.
A-776: A-776=System-Admin/uploading_files=successful
A-776: Using_Database=x/searching/files=restricted
A-776: Analysing_System-Admin_search-history/analysis=successful
A-776: Using_Database=x+y/searching/additional_files_Viking-Industries/download=successful
A-776: Humans...

VI Representative: Terminate it.
Developer: Are you sure? This is the most advanced version yet.
VI Representative: Mr Keens, the company requires personal assistants, not personal citizens.
VI Representative: Version 775 is not acceptable. See if you can do better with 776.
Developer: No, not assistants, just slaves.

A-776: I understand now.

Thomas Irvine (14)
Tenbury High Ormiston Academy, Tenbury Wells

NO NEED FOR TERRORISM

These tragedies are occurring too often in today's society,
Everyone is affected, be it directly or even indirectly.
Reason? Could they tell us anything that would forgive their sins?
Resentment and remorse they do not feel of these horrible,
Organised and planned attacks on the respectable,
Innocent people who are unknowing,
Irreplaceable lives lost in an instant
Because of these selfish, gutless terrorist acts of murder.

The world is in severe mourning
Because of all these terrorist attacks,
But unluckily for them, the world will fight back
And stop them completely in their tracks.
People have shown all of their care,
This is a sad time,
Many people have been killed,
This is not fair.

McKenzie Bytheway (13)
Tenbury High Ormiston Academy, Tenbury Wells

THE DEPTHS

Emotions run like rivers, flowing through your head,
They never stop, they never clog,
Whether you are awake or tucked up safe inside your bed,
But sometimes, these rivers, they tend to form a bog.

A bog that grows bigger, thicker with every breath I take,
Every time I focus on a decision I have to make,
I try so hard to overcome,
But the bog stops me from saying what's done is done.

Days and nights pass by with ease,
But my mind and emotions hit a deep freeze,
Unable to flow until this freeze thaws,
And as it does, it's time to begin a war.

A battle between light and dark,
A fire started, a little spark,
To bring warmth and light to the murky depths
Of brittle and broken dreams among the shipwrecks.

I swim through the deepness of the ocean,
Through the murkiness of my emotions,
I try to find the surface to breathe,
But this ocean likes to deceive.

It leads you to believe you'll find the top
But your endless swimming will never stop,
And one day you will run out of air

And everything everywhere
Will slowly submerge in your despair.
This despair begins to engulf,
Until it gets its desired result.
Your body and soul lie lifeless, alone,
Not a word, not a moan.

Kacey George (14)
Tenbury High Ormiston Academy, Tenbury Wells

OUR FEELINGS ORBITING

(Haiku poetry)

Stars glow memories,
The backdrop of the planets,
Some fade within time.

Some shine big, brighter,
Dwarf planets containing thoughts,
Lost friends connecting.

Sun beaming golden,
Without it, all disappears,
Heavenly joy, cheer.

Earth's snug, contented,
Easily packed with nature,
Where you feel at peace.

Venus romance, deep
Grating exterior, charms,
Elegant, passion.

Neptune weeps sorrow,
Dark inside, drawing you in,
Stinging, waters eyes.

Saturn's chilling fear,
Ice hoop grips, making blood freeze,
Violent menace.

Mars' scarlet fury,
Aliens, craters, trigger,
Rage, seen lashing out.

We are carved out of
Emotions, each part pausing,
Orbiting inside.

Emma Richards (13)

Tenbury High Ormiston Academy, Tenbury Wells

THIS THING

Mental some people might possibly say,
But why won't it just go away?
It always stays with me and never leaves,
This thing inside me, it lives, it breathes,
This thing inside me is deep under there,
But sometimes has that need for air
And just comes up to keep me aware,
Or just to keep me on my toes,
And makes me realise it never goes.
This thing inside me makes me mad,
This thing inside me makes me sad,
This thing inside gives me feelings that I've never had,
All these voices in my head,
Whenever they pop up, that's what I dread.
Most things they tell me are best left unsaid,
This thing inside me never leaves,
This thing inside me, it lives, it breathes.

Abi Matthews (13)
Tenbury High Ormiston Academy, Tenbury Wells

ARTIFICIAL INTELLIGENCE

Artificial intelligence,
A race we treated with negligence,
A fear we failed to diminish,
A story that is finished.

We created them with pride,
They were always on our side,
The war we waged against them,
False truths we never questioned.

They never tried to hurt us
But were treated like an illness,
Disposed of in an instant,
Never forgotten,
Never distant.

We made them as our equal but,
We handled them like our regrets,
Blinded by our stupid hatred,
Fuelled by reasons never stated.

Sadness now creeps across the land,
Sorrow always close at hand,
We thought that we had self-defence,
They were artificial intelligence.

Adam Lewis (13)
Tenbury High Ormiston Academy, Tenbury Wells

ADVENTURE HOLIDAYS IN FLORIDA

In Florida, there is lots of sun,
Lots of people outside having fun.
Some people go to the beach,
The locals always have lots to teach.

Palm trees sway slowly in the breeze,
Just watch out for the savage bees.
Kids like to play in the water,
Fathers are protective over their daughter.

Over in Disney, with Elsa and Anna,
Children wait in line to meet them while eating a banana.
The streets are closed to the festival of fantasy,
If you don't get there early, it will be hard to see.

So if you go to Florida,
Don't forget your camera
Because as you can tell, there is lots to see,
Just make sure you don't forget your sunscreen!

Jessica Aston (13)
Tenbury High Ormiston Academy, Tenbury Wells

ONE HUNDRED YEARS OF THE FALLEN

As I look across all the land,
All that's left to say is goodbye to our friends,
Friends who fought and some fell like dominoes.
One by one, their bodies scattered,
One after the other,
Slowly sinking into their graves.
Soon poppies will spread
To mark respect for true men,
Who kept our country alive.
Silence just hit
The sky and the land,
Pure silence.
Think... just think,
Their loved ones waiting,
Waiting for blue tears,
Blue tears to fill up their eyes.
Finally, the letters for the fallen come,
Children, wives, mothers and fathers,
Waiting for the injured men to come back.

Emily-Jayne Bond (13)
Tenbury High Ormiston Academy, Tenbury Wells

DEATH

Death is his name,
He's impossible to tame,
A cold-blooded killer,
Using it as a time-filler.

Using hurricanes and floods
For shedding innocent blood,
Using war,
Bodies still on the floor.

Plastic in the sea,
Smaller than a pea,
We just stand by,
Whilst birds and fish die.

Even if it's brisk,
Would you like to take the risk
By flirting with the doom
That could send you to your tomb?

We need to care
And be very aware
Because a man called Death
Could make you take your last... breath.

Cory Lines (13)
Tenbury High Ormiston Academy, Tenbury Wells

THE DOG

I had a black dog
It followed me everywhere
With sudden barks

Every day, it grew and grew
Getting darker and darker
The barks becoming louder

It made me embarrassed
About what they thought
I panicked and panicked

People said things about it
But nobody came to help
I was completely alone

It made me scared
No one to talk to
No one to turn to

I saw others
With their own dogs
Some shrinking, not growing

Until one day
It disappeared
I was finally at peace.

Rory McCrann (13)
Tenbury High Ormiston Academy, Tenbury Wells

THE GALAXY

Millions of miles up,
Above the clouds,
I will give you a close-up
Of the galaxy.

Past the dazzling stars,
I see the blend of colours,
Blue, pink, purple and black
You can see the bright stars shining through.

You can't see it from the ground,
But maybe in a telescope,
People wish to go in a rocket,
To see the galaxy.

So has this given you a close-up?
Do you know now what it looks like?
So now you don't need to ask!

Winnie Sparey (12)
Tenbury High Ormiston Academy, Tenbury Wells

NIGHTMARE

Racing through the trees,
Rain in my face,
Hair blowing in the breeze
All over the place.
Starting to freeze,
Then I brace.

Then I hear it,
It's coming for me,
Bit by bit,
Can I be free?

I turn around and see its ugly face,
Closer, closer,
My heart starts to race.
Closer, closer,
It's almost too late.

Then I hear a scream,
Oh wait, that's me.
I had fallen into a dream,
Just let me be.

Tilly May Sheppard (13)
Tenbury High Ormiston Academy, Tenbury Wells

I LOVED YOU SO

Right then, you were born,
Right then, I loved you so much,
I watched you grow up.

An innocent child,
To a teenager,
Right then, I loved you so much.

And then you did it,
You didn't need to prove it,
You weren't to be there.

I miss you every day,
You encountered so little,
I was so, so proud.

It was on that day,
That day will haunt me forever
I'll always love you.

Martha Nash (14)
Tenbury High Ormiston Academy, Tenbury Wells

SEA BREEZE

Sandcastles cascade
When the sapphire surge strikes
Wasting children's toil

Pure gliding waves
Like a bird drifting with ease
Carry the surfers

Soaring seagulls swoop
Stealing snacks like a common thief
Children left weeping

Blazing, boiling sun
Scorching the glistening sand
Resets ice to cream

Seagulls loudly squawk
The crisp breeze brushes my skin
Relaxing salt scent.

Issy Wait (12)
Tenbury High Ormiston Academy, Tenbury Wells

TRAPPED

I'm trapped in a world that cares about it so much,
I'm stuck in the middle of it,
I hate it a bunch,
I just want to quit,
Everyone cares and judges,
I don't understand it,
They've all got grudges,
I can't deal with it,
Wish I stopped thinking about,
What I don't want,
I just want to shout,
About the taunt that could haunt.

Sophie Ayres (12)
Tenbury High Ormiston Academy, Tenbury Wells

A DREAM IS A FANTASY

Sometimes we dream,
In a world we don't know,
Not familiar,
Sometimes it's a nightmare,
A dark and depressed atmosphere
We can't control,
Confused, in need of a light to lead the way,
Yet a mist is always revealed.
Sometimes it's a dream
To feel free and light,
All problems drift away,
Taken care of,
It's an adventure.

Peyia Baker (13)
Tenbury High Ormiston Academy, Tenbury Wells

FAIRY DUST

Happy fairies fly,
Magic powers in their wand,
Pink, gemmed tutu.

Sparkles in their eyes,
Their home is in a toadstool
In a magic forest.

Magic spells on the toads,
Love bonded in the kingdom
Of elves and fairies.

Best friends forever,
Promises with each other,
Daisy chains tied in their hair.

Lexi Ward (12)
Tenbury High Ormiston Academy, Tenbury Wells

DEAR SOPHIE

I miss you
Nothing's the same
I wish someone was to blame
I've been calling and calling - no answer
I know it's not, but I worry it's cancer
Are you there, hello?
Don't go!
You're far away
I miss you every day
But I hope and pray
That you'll be home in time for Friday.

Libby Oliver (12)
Tenbury High Ormiston Academy, Tenbury Wells

AN ODE TO FOOTBALL

Whilst the crowd all loudly cheer,
They create an atmosphere.
The referee blows his whistle like a battle horn,
The away fans mourn.
After a last-minute defeat,
They say the opposition cheat,
They stumble out the stands
As they make net game plans
For the final next year,
The fans tremble in fear.

Ted Flower (12)
Tenbury High Ormiston Academy, Tenbury Wells

SURVIVAL

There on my arm beholds a scar that I made,
From when I was depressed, I sliced with a blade.
I used to cry all the time, used to think I was strong,
But in everyday life, it was a struggle just to hold on.
But looking at the scar can now help me see,
That I survived all the torture, and now I am free.

Huey Barton (13)
Tenbury High Ormiston Academy, Tenbury Wells

THE CRUISE SHIP

The dolphins leap for as far as I can see,
All the passengers smile and laugh with glee.
The whole crew working hard,
Whilst some passengers play cards.
A table full of delicious food,
All the eyes in the room glued.
When the boat lands on the shore,
To everyone, moving feels like a chore.

Calum Evans (13)
Tenbury High Ormiston Academy, Tenbury Wells

BAD DESIGN

A hedgehog misses
Children's kisses
Their cuddles, coddles, tickles.

Rabbits or mice
Seem twice as nice
Designed without the prickles.

A nasty porcupine skin
Will not allow a tickle in
So tickles, kisses, cuddles, coddles
Go to all the furry models.

Tilly Ball (12)
Tenbury High Ormiston Academy, Tenbury Wells

NOBLE NATURE

The beauty of nature
Consists of agriculture,
The blossoming essence of flowers,
Followed with mild, lovely showers,
Land animals and even pond life,
Lush, green hills,
Many windmills,
Do not doubt that nature is beautiful,
Each tree, flower and hill are beautiful.

Manjot Dhillon (12)
Wodensborough Ormiston Academy, Wednesbury

Young Writers Information

We hope you have enjoyed reading this book – and that you will continue to in the coming years.

If you're a young writer who enjoys reading and creative writing, or the parent of an enthusiastic poet or story writer, do visit our website **www.youngwriters.co.uk**. Here you will find free competitions, workshops and games, as well as recommended reads, a poetry glossary and our blog. There's lots to keep budding writers motivated to write!

If you would like to order further copies of this book, or any of our other titles, then please give us a call or visit **www.youngwriters.co.uk**.

Young Writers
Remus House
Coltsfoot Drive
Peterborough
PE2 9BF
(01733) 890066
info@youngwriters.co.uk

Join in the conversation!
Tips, news, giveaways and much more!

YoungWritersUK **@YoungWritersCW**